Who gives a Hoot?

Do you?

Anne Mangan

Text copyright © 2022 by Anne Mangan

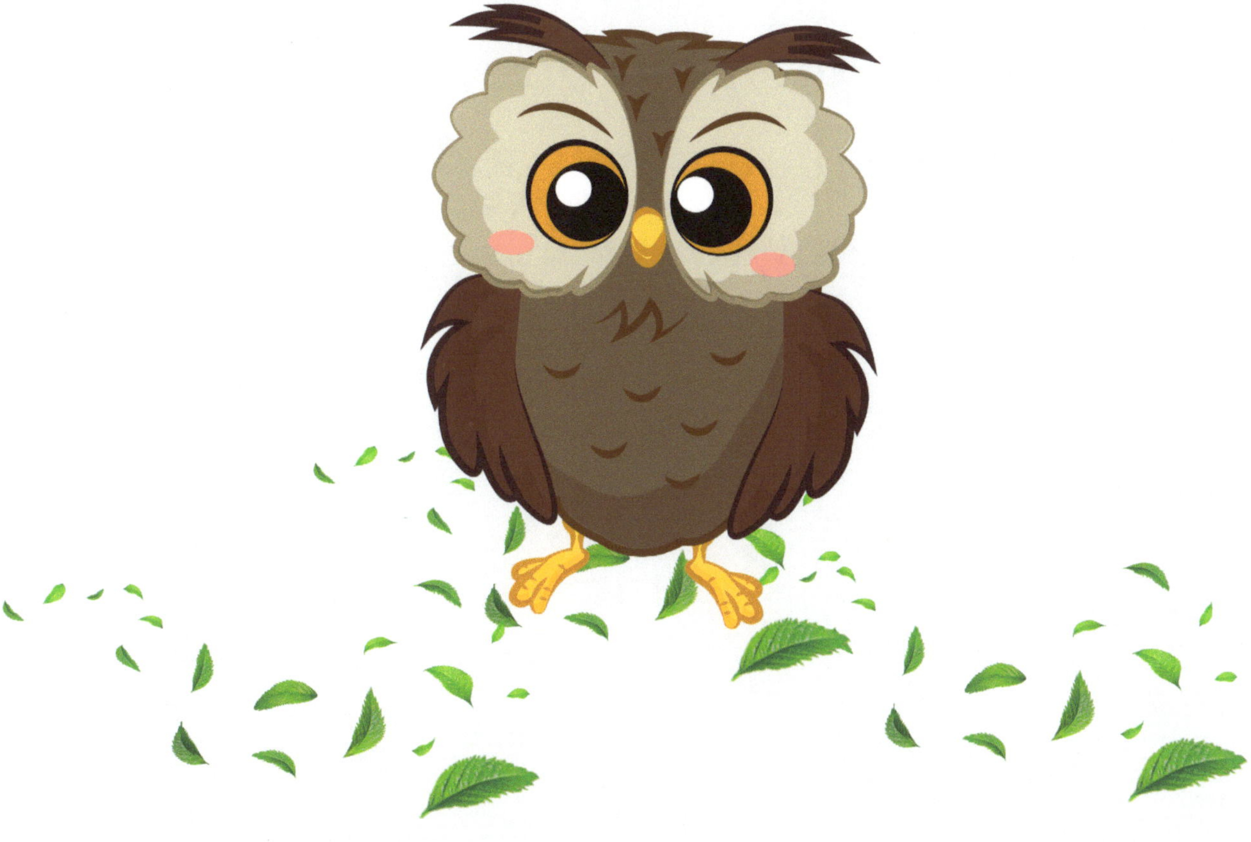

This book is dedicated to all
the children who give a hoot
about the animals and the
environment.

The animals were worried, that the
humans didn't care.
About the Earth, which living things,
are all supposed to share.

Screeched Owl "I give a hoot"
his wings flapping about.
"That electric power could,
eventually run out."

The animals agreed,
"The humans just can't see."
"We'd be alright, but they'd,
be lost, without phones and TV."

"And what about computers?"
said Dodo with a wink.
"They'll have to use their brains,
if computers are extinct."

"Where will I get my leaves"
piped up Koala bear.
"If there's no trees" Sloth yawned,
"I'll have to get a chair."

Then Kangaroo hopped up,
with rubbish in her pouch.
"Seeing litter" Joey said,
"Makes my Mum, such a grouch."

Monkey, as he swung in,
asked "What about the trees."

'There'll be nowhere to put
our hives"
buzzed the busy bees.

"And what if there's no water"
said camel with a grump.
"The humans will get thirsty,
not me, I have two humps."

The animals then thought,
of not taking a bath.
In unison, they all went "Yuck"
which made them start to laugh.

Just as they were laughing,
some kids who looked like you.
Came up, and asked the animals,
"Can we, give a hoot too."

"We know ways you can help"
the animals all said.
We've got a lot of great ideas,
from all the books we've read.

"They played a game where rubbish,
was put into the bin.
The kids teamed up with Kangaroo,
to make sure they would win.

They checked the taps were off,
made sure they didn't drip.

And tried, to not use plastic bags,
on their shopping trip.

They turned off their computers,
and even their TVs.

And went outside to exercise,
as well as hug some trees.

The kids made all these changes,
and the animals then knew.

Some humans, give a hoot.

And, we hope that you will too.

www.ingramcontent.com/pod-product-compliance
Lightning Source LLC
Chambersburg PA
CBHW042131110726
48006CB00003B/840